# From The Shattered Shell

Michaela Perrigo

Made with ❤ on the BookLeaf Publishing Platform
www.bookleafpub.in
www.bookleafpub.com

# Dedication

To the broken pieces, may you create your masterpiece with brilliance and warmth.

# Preface

Dear reader,


Use caution.
The contents of this collection may be sharp, scalding,
and unstomachable.


For those who crave the sourness of lemons and being
ripped to shreds, take care of yourself.
This book is not for the meek and feeble. Rage through it.
And rage again.


When you reach the end, breathe and admire your
collection of scars. Then, reimagine them. Reshape them.
And prove yourself the masterpiece you always knew
you were.

# Acknowledgements

Thank you to everyone who encouraged me and kept me going. Thank you to those who caused me pain for I found beauty in it as I reshaped the words thrown at me into my identity. Thank you to Ms. Hord and Ms. Harriger for pushing me towards poetry and helping me breathe life into the broken pieces. Thank you to Cassey and my mom for putting up with thousands of 3am messages that were just snippets of a poem I needed to share. Thank you to BookLeaf Publishing for allowing me to get a foot in the door and share my hopes with the world.

# 1. Deals with the Devil

Do you recognize me
Old friend

I
Who lives in your eyes
Making them
Farther away
Dry and dark
Unfeeling
To all emotions

Do you know my voice
Sweet one

Words
Kept crammed together
Spoken
Quick and soft
Knowing
No one is really truly listening

Do you know the scent
Dear child

Death
And blood
Spiraling into the drain
Among steam
And hot water
Jetting itself through your skin
Red and raw

Do you recognize me
My face

Lonely and lovely
Scared and scarred
Staring with sullen sunken eyes
Devoid of all emotions
Black shadows
Casting themselves
Into the hollows of your cheeks
The pale skin tone
standing out against blood
And dripping mascara

Those eyes
Can you see me yet child
I'm right here
I never left you
My darling

Because
As you know
I
Am the only thing
To truly love you

Look closer
In that mirror
I am there
In the skin
Stretched taut across
Ribs, pelvis, scapula

I am there
In the hair
Stringy and dripping down
The pale slopes of your body

I am there
In every single thing
That makes you

# 2. 11/26/24 10:35pm

I think my bed has finally merged with me
You see
I am shackled to it
It's foam topper
Quietly meshing with my skin

I sit
On top
All day long

I work in bed
Eat in bed
Sleep (sometimes on the couch) but mostly in bed

I rarely leave my bed
But
I was hungry tonight
And so the beast craving sustenance
What else was I to do
So I left my bed
peeling the sheets away as if it were my own flesh
And went foraging

The rot has won again

I find
When I reach the kitchen
The food is scarce
And ever more scarce
Is the spoons to cook

So I try to make Kraft Mac and cheese
The spiral kind
I work diligently
Collecting my supplies
Filling the pot with water
Boiling it
Stirring the pasta
Draining it
Mixing the crappy cheese sauce
And...
It's expired
Like a month ago expired

So what else can I do
I throw out the spoiled food
And
I go back to my bed
And I sit there
I can't sleep because I'm hungry
Can't eat because all the food is old or out

And I just sit in bed
Surrounded by all this
And
I'm still
And calm
And numb

Because what else can I do
How else can I try to fight the rot
I can't
It's finally succeeded at destroying me from both ends

And so
I sink back into my bed
Feel the sheets layer onto my flesh
Feel the foam envelop me from below
Merge to my body
Making me just a little more bed than me

The rot
Sinks its claws deeper
And I sigh as my bones creak
And settle
Into the home that never left

And the rot
Breathes

# 3. Lemons

Someone told me once that I looked like the kind of girl
who would go dancing in the middle of a busy
intersection.
That's when I realized it wasn't so much in my head
anymore.
That it was dripping from my lips like lemon juice
Sour and clear
Choking on the seeds and gnawing the rind
And I'm calling out for water
Because my mouth is bone dry
But everyone around me just stares and says
"Just stop eating the lemon"
"Don't complain when you don't try to fix it"
And that was the best advice I ever got about my
depression.

# 4. Mama

They say he ruptured my ovary mama
That I need surgery
The hospital
The doctors told me
I have a concussion
And fractures on my skull
Eye socket
A split lip
Mama

He was in the military mama
I thought that meant he was safe
Mama
He told me to relax
I don't think I'll ever relax again
Mama

Bruises scatter my skin now mama
Dark like his skin
I need to get my car mama
From the place where it happened
I parked next to him
I just want to go home
Bathe my skin in alcohol

Inside and out

Mama
Do you think I'll ever be clean again
They tell me they'll sedate me mama
I'm scared of the dark now
That split second when he hit me
And the lights went out
Taunting my mentals
Mama

Did you hear me cry for you
He ripped my insides
Tore my flesh
Stole my innocence and trust
Mama

I tried to be brave
But somewhere I wandered off
The tears soaked my shirt

They needed my shirt for the tests
It was my favorite

Mama

Can you find a replacement
Without the stain of memory

# 5. "But I loved him"

Then hate him.
Buy a dartboard and tape his picture onto it and hate him.
But do not acknowledge his existence in a spiteful text or tweet.
Because to acknowledge that you hate him is to acknowledge that you loved him and that he broke you with the permission of your smile.
And it will satisfy him in a way that boys who speak in cruel tongues get off on.
Do not acknowledge your spite with the world because the world only sees a weakness to prey off of.
Acknowledge your spite for your own wellbeing and hate with a heart who has known love because only then will it mend itself with the ferociousness of lions and not just that of a sweet cub.

# 6. Winter

Crystallized sugar blankets every surface
a smooth baby skin covering
shrinking back
slinking away from the sunshine smile of children

The impressionable snow giving way to footsteps
and paw prints
the white flawless mounds
making music as pieces of itself drip into oblivion
the ground accepting the cold frozenness of the
elemental molecules
as the winter sunshine slips out from behind the horizon
frigid air laden with the moisture slipping from the
ground's grasp
sunshine that is both tropical and glacial
children watch the snow disappearing:
watch the army of snowmen littering their street
melt.

Watch the igloos become anthills until even the anthills
are gone.
The snow angels seem to be the first to go;
matching the faith of religion.
When it's so cold and you wonder,

how could this snow disappear?
This little miracle for the southern states
leave?
This childlike innocence of weather;
both deadly and welcomed
Why is this half frozen water so special?
How could it possibly become so perfect?

And then the perfection slips away,
almost overnight...
and no one really recognizes the disappearance
until
one day it's just gone.

Completely melted
and we're left waiting for the next snowfall
like leaping off a precipice
and praying for something to catch you.

# 7. Christmas Serenade

December 21, 2018


It's amazing how much of a house you can see with the
front door wide open
Gaping like a toothless grin full of warm white light
Perhaps music plays out
Or more likely the sound of a TV show no one is
watching

You can see
At this time of year
The Christmas lights hanging from the doorway
Perhaps a half-decorated Christmas tree
Children littering the floor in front of it
The adults laughing and carrying on in the kitchen
Just out of view or walking past the doorway
With some sort of wine sloshing from their cups

A smell
Of gingerbread and cider
Cookies and peppermint
Wafting out into the street
Perhaps smoke reaching upwards from the roof
Barely visible with all the lights

Turn slightly and a giant Santa
Obstructs your view
A glow of more lights outlining him
To be a dark shadow around the edges

This is how you continue
Through the neighborhoods
Admiring lights
And the wafting smells reach out to your nose
Enveloping you in warmth
Despite the cold almost snow weather

Then
Like a gaping hole among the bright stars
A blackened lot
Visible only by the sunbeams surrounding
An admonished place
Hardly a home
The darkness so thick

This
Is how the neighborhood looks
All the rest of the year

# 8. Mantra #1

You will be okay again
you have to breathe
rinse the salt from your face
ignore that pain in your stomach
remember this is temporary
Don't fight for those who don't belong
you are okay
remember this
and breathe

# 9. Thunder Breaks

It stormed tonight

I saw the lightning flash in your eyes
Heard the thunder rumble in your voice
Those warning sirens going off 30 seconds before impact

Your fist to my jawline
Wind whipping through my hair
As the heat of contact soared through my face

Trees uprooted in the glimpse of an eye
Foundations broken and lonely
Wishing for the walls they once found comfort and
safeness in

The storm worsening
Seeming like it'd never pass by
Wondering if it was worth waiting out
In the storm shelter I built for myself
Far beneath the walls you were tearing at

# 10. Seasons of You

**I. FALL**

When fall leaves fell
I fell into you.
Your arms like an oversized sweater
Enveloping me,
In warmth and comfort

**II. WINTER**

Now winter is here
And it is 78 degrees and sunny
And the fire that burns in our embrace
And kisses
are scalding my skin raw
But I don't feel the pain
I only see the beauty of your colors licking up towards
me.

**III. SPRING**

The dew on the grass stops freezing
And the birds start coming alive with song
But without you

All I can see is the rain
And all I can feel is the draft from my window
That you promised to fix
But never did
I guess you promised to fix a lot of things

## IV. SUMMER

In summer the heatwave melted the memories of you
Like a kid's popsicle
In the family park
And I thrive
On the buzz
And the fun
That accompanies the warmth

## V. THE STORM

Every year I swear to myself
That this will be the year,
The year that I will never write another poem about you
The year that my life won't come crashing back down
To memories of you
And every year
Something happens
And you're back
Crashing into my life

Acting as a tidal wave
On the cities of my oceanic being
And every time you're gone
I'm left pulling pieces of myself
From the unforgiving seas
Rebuilding myself until next year.

Hurricanes are so much sweeter than tidal waves.
Because when the hurricane is gone the sun will help
you rebuild.
You can find the missing pieces of yourself two blocks
down.
But with the tidal wave,
The tidal wave breaks pieces of you off
And carry them back to the sea
Holding them above their head
As a trophy
Of the destruction they caused.

# 11. Solar Flares

I'm in love with the sun
some might say it's inappropriate
but I can't seem to stop it

When I see him
I glow
and people say how beautiful I look
basking in his glow

He creates art in the sky
his use of color to complement my eyes
his goodnight text to me every night
and the good morning to start my day

When he's near I can feel his arms snake around my
waist pulling me tight to him
his fingers trailing further
My body responding immediately
curling and twisting towards his beams

I can feel it when he's missing too
its harder to breathe
and I search for a break in the clouds
to be loved by him

And then
so quick I might have blinked
he reappears
and as he scoops me up
my body is no longer mine to control

# 12. Love Song

In may of 2022
I came home with a buzzing in my ears
Like a distant cicada
on a warm summer afternoon

Melting frozen yogurt
And awkward friendly touches
Dancing around each other
As young love blossoms do

June of 2022
The sun beat down
Tan brown skin
And warm summers evenings
Made way for a first romance
And long embrace
Car rides for the first time
And a prolonged detour to goodbye again

July, august, and September
Came and flew by
With visits lasting months
And dreams lasting within it

October came and together at last
Living like lovers
Hoping time wouldn't pass

November
Like a freight train moves
Went by just as fast
And I found that that buzzing had turned to twinkling
chimes

December 14th
We pledged our love
And the dreams of the future
Were carved into marble sculptures
A bust of our love
Held dear to my heart

And now in September
We reaffirm we will last
And that buzzing that once was
Has turned into a sonnet of our love

As sonnets turn to symphonies
Our love will only grow
Through hardships and triumphs

We reach the finish line

And still our love shall never peak
But continue growing through the coming years

By movie marathons
And 2am Waffle House dates
Mini golf and skee ball tournaments
Through laughter and tears
And jokes for only our own ears

We will grow into an orchestra of love
That holds the final note dear
I love you for forever
And even that's too soon

For this orchestra of love
Plays only on for you

# 13. Sun Daze

I want to sit on a strip of beach
between two oceans
lapping towards me
but not quite reaching

I want the sun to be warm
and the sky, blue
a light breeze
not enough to make the sand into weapons

The sand soft
and warm
not digging into my skin

I
will lounge
perfectly still
hair cascading around me
a beautiful dark body
laying alone
on this island of beach

And this is how I will love myself
And this is how you will never reach me

Because you
Could not swim my depths

# 14. Sea Salt and Cigarettes

Smells like sea salt and cigarettes
taste like crystalized sugar water
a little gritty but so sweet

Traces of nicotine on my fingertips
electrifying your skin with every caress

I will wrap this sweater
tighter to my skin
hoping to keep out the cold
while you make up your mind

Instead
I will watch the earth move
and the stars glimmer
and the moon disappear and reappear

# 15. Coffeehouse Daydreams

The coffee shop was empty
and you smiled
over the lip of your coffee mug
the steam cascading around your face
giving an air of mystery

I saw the dust motes
floating and flickering
like tiny embers
in the sunlight
streaming through the window
and I could feel my entire reality shift

# 16. Man Eater

What I love about first dates
Is not the excitement and nervousness
Melding together
And taunting every nerve ending

It's the way a man looks at you
Slowly unraveling you with their mind
The way they become obsessed
Enraptured
With the way your tongue flicks between your lips
And the ice cream drips down your hand
The way you twist your head for a better angle

Their eyes locked on you
The words stumbling and stalling
As they become entranced with your actions
The way you can smile slyly and cause them to drop
their breath dangerously low
How you have them wrapped around your finger
And they don't even notice

Because the subtleties that make a female soft
Are also a poison to ensnare their minds
They are almost always on their best behavior

But test the boundaries
But you are in
Complete
Control
They are addicted to you
From the way you blink
To the way you wipe your lip from the stickiness

That's the real reason
First dates are empowering

That man
For a period of time
Breathes only your air
Expelled from your lungs
And by the end of it
They beg for more
Not noticing how the carbon dioxide numbs them and
their head pounds
They are entranced
Entrapped
And loving it

That is when I devour them

# 17. P.I.S.K.C.L.T.L

*(piss-kil-tul)*

Poetry,
in the sweetest of forms,
should rip your soul to pieces,
knock the breath from your lungs,
crush your beating life force to silence,
leave you clutching the shards
that were broken off back into you.
Like your will alone could pull you back together.

Poetry,
in the bitterest of forms,
soaks sunshine through your skin,
kisses you sweetly, but desperately,
causes your heart to beat sporadically,
leaves you high on happiness,
the kind that glows, glitters, and glides.
Like honey is dripping onto everything bitter and black.

# 18. Ode to Who I Hope to Become

I want to sit awake at night and forget who I am because I'm talking to someone else who gets it without saying a word. I want to look up into the night sky and not see millions of unwanted and unknown dreams cast aside by wonder less spirits. I want to be able to count the colors in someone's laughter and see the thoughts in how they hold themselves. I want to teach someone how to be comfortable without fear. I don't want to recognize myself when I look in a mirror, I've grown too comfortable with how things were. I want to walk to the beach and sit in the sand and think about how similar everything is to what was. I want to be able to cut people out of my life like I was born sharp-edged and not as thin as paper leaves falling from snipped wings. I want to cascade, not like smoke, but like fog. Gently gliding over every surface without reaction when cars come barreling through me. I want to be as mysterious as the sun because whoever stares long enough will be blinded by the fact, they thought they knew my shape. I will be more than you ever thought I could be and when you try to take credit for only the good, I will point you in the direction I have come.

# 19. 6/18/19

Orange glow
fire on waters
churning
with a crippling weight
of sorrow
and pain

Alone on the brink of existence
plunging into cold waters
of delusional faith

A grayish green
instead of stark blue
Reminding us what summer feels like
through the sight of orange flames

And then
rising through the strange gray smoky haze
of the remains of a storm

A yellow flicker faint
and unwavering
standing steadfast

above the murky waters
and all the suffocating vapors

# 20. Sand Castles

When the sand gives instead of the shell breaking

I pull the shell out of the hole it has formed
Brush the sand from its edges and crevices
Place it softly in a new, safer place

I tell the shell how proud I am of its ability
To withstand whatever someone places on it
The success is there
But I know what a struggle it was

I remind this shell
That although it has been strong
It is also okay to have some cracks
Whether they're microscopic or visible to anyone who
looks
It doesn't lessen the success in surviving

When the shell breaks instead of the sand giving in

I pick up the broken shards
Carefully piece them together
A feeble attempt at repairing the damage

I tell the shell it is okay
That things can become better
That this is not the end of its story
After all, sand is made up of the broken pieces of trillions
of shells
How strong must they be to not give in

I remind this shell
That it is not a failure
For cracking under the weight of a foot
Another person is a lot to carry when it's all on you

As I look at the sandcastles around me
Billions of tiny shell particles
Balancing and blending together
To form a stable monument

I am reminded
Of the strength of broken pieces

# 21. Catch and Release a.k.a. End of Life Planning and Arrangements

When I die
Do not bury me
I do not wish for my bones to mix with the soil
I do not care to sprout flowers and trees from my broken decayed pieces
I do not want to grow taller and reach towards the sky
Only to be chopped down and plucked out of my home again
I do not want to wander through the gravestones for eternity
I've had enough of that in life

Instead
Burn my remains
Crush my bones into powder
Chip down my teeth and disintegrate my hair
Unrecognizable to anyone but my own atoms reaching towards one another

Store me in a ziplock
A brown wooden box plain and barely larger than the

melody box I used to own
(The chipped pieces of my existence rattling inside may
sound just the same)
A small but appropriate and tastefully plain urn
I do not need the jewels and embellishments
I am dead

Travel with me
In that inoffensive container
Buy me a seat on a plane
Strap me in
Transport me home again

To the sea
Any coast will do just fine
Swim into those waters with me
Hold me close for just a moment
And release me back to where I once came from
Let me swim into the depths
Make friends with the sea creatures
Be made into homes by coral reefs
Or microorganisms

When I have sank away from you
Back towards the comfort of the depths
Do not cry for me
Your tears can not mix with the saltwater coursing

through my fragmented reality

Instead
Leap from the water
Spray droplets as wide and high as they can go
Scream into the horizon and know
Somewhere deep within the depths
I am home
Again

When you believe that you miss me
Visit me by the seaside
Feel how I caress your toes as you look out to the
horizon
And get stuck in tendrils of your hair as the wind moves
me

And when you're ready finally
To meet me again
Watch for rain
I'll be there every time
And I will show you how the world catches you
And releases you
Back into the depths of home

www.ingramcontent.com/pod-product-compliance
Lightning Source LLC
LaVergne TN
LVHW041242200726
843507LV00013B/2777